King Tut
Tales from the Tomb
by Diana C. Briscoe

Reading Consultant:
Timothy Rasinski, Ph.D.
Professor of Reading Education
Kent State University

Content Consultant:
Fred Poyner
Art Historian
Specialist in Egyptian
Paintings and Sculpture

Red Brick™ Learning

Published by Red Brick™ Learning
7825 Telegraph Road, Bloomington, Minnesota 55438
http://www.redbricklearning.com

Library of Congress Cataloging-in-Publication Data
Briscoe, Diana, 1949–
    King Tut: tales from the tomb/by D.C. Briscoe: reading consultant,
Timothy Rasinski.
        p. cm.—(High five reading)
        Summary: Discusses ancient Egyptian customs and beliefs regarding death
and the afterlife, the process of mummification, and the legend of a
mummy's curse in relation to the discovery of King Tut's tomb in 1922.
Includes bibliographical references (p. 46) and index.
        ISBN-13: 978-0-7368-9553-8 (Hardcover)
        ISBN-10: 0-7368-9553-1 (Hardcover)
        ISBN-13: 978-0-7368-9531-6 (Paperback)
        ISBN-10: 0-7368-9531-0 (Paperback)
        1. Tutankhamen, King of Egypt—Tomb—Juvenile literature. 2. Funeral
rites and ceremonies—Egypt—Juvenile literature. [1. Tutankhamen, King
of Egypt—Tomb. 2. Kings, queens, rulers, etc. 3. Egypt—Antiquities.
4. Egypt—Civilization—To 332 B.C. 5. Funeral rites and ceremonies—Egypt.]
I. Title. II. Series.
DT87.5 .B669 2002
932'.014'092—dc21
                                        2002000188

Created by Kent Publishing Services, Inc.
Executive Editor: Robbie Butler
Designed by Signature Design Group, Inc.

Photo Credits:
Page 5, Stapleton Collection/Corbis; page 7, Fulvio Roiter/Corbis; pages 9, 17,
43, Roger Wood/Corbis; pages 11, 18, 19, 20, 23, 35, 40 (top and bottom),
Bettmann/Corbis; page 15, Archivo Iconografico, S.A./Corbis; pages 24, 36,
Charles & Josette Lenars/Corbis; page 28, Gianni Dagli Orti/Corbis; page 31,
Historical PictureArchive/Corbis; page 32, Sandro Vannini/Corbis

Printed in the United States of America in Stevens Point, Wisconsin.
052013   007400CPS

Table of Contents

Chapter 1

"Wonderful Things!"

More than 3,000 years ago, a king died in Egypt. Over the years, the king's tomb became buried. It was not discovered until less than 100 years ago. What do you think was discovered there?

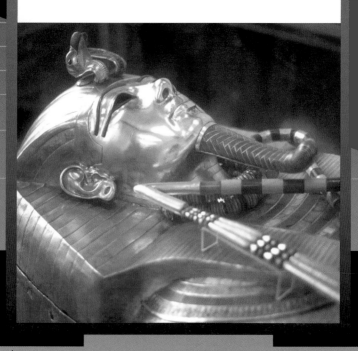

"Can You See Anything?"

It is November 26, 1922. A group of people stand at the end of a narrow hall. The hall had been buried for thousands of years. A little in front of them, a man named Howard Carter holds a candle. The man is looking through a small hole in a doorway.

"Can you see anything?" a voice calls out from the group. It is Lord Carnarvon (carn-AH-von). "Wonderful things!" replies Carter. His years of labor have paid off. He has found the lost tomb of a pharaoh.

Howard Carter explores part of the newly discovered tomb.

tomb: a grave, room, or building for holding a dead body
pharaoh: a king of ancient Egypt

Digging in Egypt

Both Carnarvon and Carter had been to Egypt before. Carnarvon first came in 1903. For health reasons, he needed to escape the damp English winters. He was rich and enjoyed archeology (ar-kee-OL-uh-jee). He decided to get involved in this interest. Carter, an English archeologist, had been working in Egypt since 1892.

In 1907, Carter and Carnarvon teamed up. They dug at Thebes, an ancient city on the Nile River. Here they found many tombs and two lost temples. They also dug at two other sites, but found little.

In 1914, they returned to Thebes. They wanted to dig in an area called the Valley of the Kings. There, Carter found the looted tomb of a pharaoh. But from 1917 to 1922, he found nothing else important.

---

damp: wet or moist
archeology: the study of the past by looking at old buildings and other objects
looted: when valued objects have been stolen from their owners

Just in Time!

The Valley of the Kings got its name for the many pharaohs buried there. Several people had dug there before Carter. They said there was nothing left to find.

In 1922, Carnarvon was ready to give up. Then his luck turned. On November 4, Carter found the first step of a staircase. At the bottom was a closed door. A symbol on the door showed the name of a pharaoh— Tut-ankh-Amun (toot-ank-AH-moon).

Visitors wait to enter the tomb of a pharaoh in Egypt.

More Closed Doors

On November 25, Carter's workmen broke open the door. Rubble filled the hallway inside. At first, they thought someone had robbed the tomb.

The next morning, the workers cleared some of the rubble. They found a second door. The door had been broken open and rebuilt in the past.

Carter knocked a small hole through this door. He lit a candle and looked in. He could see a small room. Furniture, chests, and other treasures filled the room. Maybe robbers had been there. But they had left plenty behind!

The next day, the men opened the door. Carter and Carnarvon went in. To the left, they found a door to another room full of treasure. To the right, life-size statues guarded yet another door. This door led to Tut-ankh-Amun's burial chamber.

---

rubble: a mixture of earth and stones
burial chamber: a room for a dead body and its coffin

What Was in There?

A few days later, Carter and Carnavon entered the burial chamber. Inside they found wall paintings. One showed the great men of Egypt dragging a sled to a tomb. On the sled was the body of a young king. Other paintings showed the Egyptian gods welcoming Tut-ankh-Amun to his new life. In the chamber, they later found Tut-ankh-Amun's solid gold coffin.

To one side of the chamber was yet another room. It held a shrine and still more treasure. A statue of Anubis (a-NEW-bis), the jackal god, guarded this shrine. Around the shrine stood the statues of four goddesses.

Anubis, the jackal god

shrine: any site or structure used in worship or devotion
jackal: a wild animal related to the dog

9

Wild Excitement

Carter made front-page news around the world. He gathered a team of experts. Together, they emptied the tomb and studied the items. It took them 10 years to carefully remove and record everything from the tomb. They counted thousands of items.

Study, not Looting

To make money, most early archeologists sold the treasures they found. But Carter belonged to a new group of archeologists. These scientists did not want to loot the treasure. They wanted to work with the Egyptians to learn about their past.

So who was this boy-king Carter found? What was his life like? Read on to find out about the most famous of all pharaohs, the one we call "King Tut."

The throne of King Tut is removed from the tomb in this 1923 photo.

— CHAPTER 2 —

Pharaoh of Egypt

King Tut was only 9 years old when he became pharaoh. He died when he was 17. But for eight years, King Tut ruled Egypt. What was life like for this boy-king?

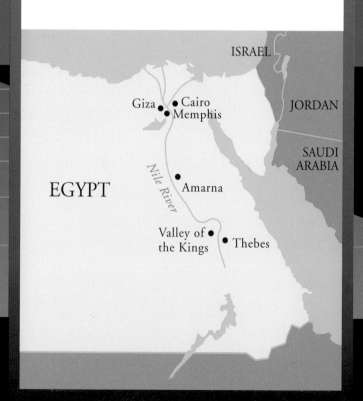

ISRAEL

JORDAN

SAUDI ARABIA

Giza • • Cairo
• Memphis

EGYPT

Nile River

• Amarna

Valley of • • Thebes
the Kings

The 18th Dynasty

King Tut came from a line of pharaohs called the 18th Dynasty. These pharaohs built a great empire that stretched from modern Syria to the south of the Sudan. Memphis was the center of the empire.

King Tut was the son of King Akh-en-Aten (AH-ken-ah-ten). Tut's father made great changes to the empire. For hundreds of years, the empire and its rulers had worshiped many gods. The sun-god Amen-Ra had become the most important. But Tut's father worshiped only one god. This was a new sun-god called "Aten." So Tut's father closed the temples of Amen-Ra and all the other gods. He also took the priests' great riches away.

Then King Akh-en-Aten moved his government away from Memphis. He built a new city called Amarna. Tut was born there.

Because King Akh-en-Aten worshiped Aten, he named his son "Tut-ankh-Aten." The young Tut worshiped as his father did.

dynasty: a series of rulers who belong to the same family
empire: a country ruled by an emperor

A Pharaoh's Role

People believed the pharaohs were living gods. They also believed the other gods listened to the pharaoh. So the pharaoh connected his people and the gods.

Each year, the pharaoh would ask the gods for the Nile River flood to come. If there was no flood, there was no water to grow crops. Then people starved.

Pharaohs did not do much work themselves. They had servants called *scribes*. The scribes did much of the work.

Tut's father also had help from two in-laws. Ay organized the government. Hor-em-heb was his army commander. These two in-laws did their best to keep things running smoothly.

---

scribe: an educated man who could read and write

Emergency Action

Soon after his father died, Tut became king in 1336 B.C. But Ay began to make big changes, for Tut and for Egypt. He brought Tut back to Memphis from Amarna. Then Ay planned a marriage between Tut and an older relative.

Ay also reopened Amen-Ra's temples. He brought back the old religion. Things changed back to the way they had been.

Statue of King Akh-en-Aten, the father of King Tut

15

Life for King Tut

King Tut was young. But he was old enough to understand what Ay was doing. He could see that Ay was undoing changes his father had made. But Tut did not have the power to stop him. Tut could not even leave Memphis and return to the city his father had built.

Tut heard the priests of Amen-Ra call his father a criminal. Remember, Tut's father had closed the temples of the other gods. He had taken the priests' riches. He had worshiped the sun-god Aten, not the sun-god Amen-Ra. So the priests had not liked him.

Young King Tut listened while Ay and other officials spoke for him. Ay wanted Egypt to be strong. He probably helped Tut make decisions about the empire.

Ay even changed Tut-ankh-Aten's name to Tut-ankh-Amun. Can you tell why?

---

criminal: a person who breaks the laws of the country

A Short Life

We know very little about King Tut's life. But from his tomb we do have clues about things he might have enjoyed.

He may have liked outdoor sports. There were six chariots in his tomb. A gold shrine shows Tut shooting birds with a bow and arrows. A box shows him watching while servants fish with nets.

King Tut may also have liked games. Carter found six sets of game boards in Tut's tomb. There were bows and arrows for hunting. There were also armor, shields, swords, daggers, and other weapons. His hobbies were normal for the time.

This scene of a pharaoh riding a chariot into battle was painted on a casket of King Tut.

An Early Death

No one is sure how King Tut died. X rays of Tut's skull show a sliver of bone inside his brain. He may have been killed by a blow to the head. But if he was killed, it's not clear who did it.

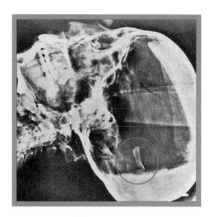

An X ray of King Tut's head shows a sliver of bone inside his brain.

When Tut died, he left no son. Ay and Hor-em-heb had to find a new pharaoh. Ay decided to take power. He became pharaoh. He did this by marrying Tut's widow. Ay only ruled four years. Then Hor-em-heb took over the empire.

When a pharaoh died, the Egyptians treated the body in a special way. They made it into a mummy. Any ideas how they did this?

---

widow: a woman whose husband has died

Hor-em-heb, in the tomb painting above, took over the empire five years after the death of King Tut.

— CHAPTER **3** —

Making a Mummy

When pharaohs died they got special treatment. They had special tombs filled with many treasures. Their bodies also received special care. They were turned into mummies. Below, a modern artist tried to show how Egyptians made a mummy. In this chapter, learn how they were really made.

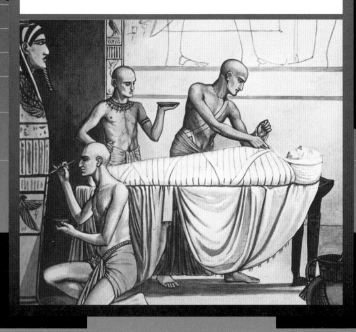

A No-brainer

In ancient Egypt, embalmers prepared a dead person for burial. This process took 70 days. Egyptian embalmers used this process to make a mummy of King Tut's body.

Inside a special tent, called an *ibu*, the embalmers first cleaned the body. They washed the body with natron mixed with Nile River water.

Next, they took the body to a workshop called a *wabet*. There the embalmers removed many of the body's organs. They started with the brain. They pushed a large hook up the body's nose to get at the brain. Ancient Egyptians thought the brain was not important. So they scooped the brain out in pieces and threw it away.

---

embalmer: in ancient Egypt, a person who makes a mummy
burial: the placing of a dead body in its final resting place
natron: a natural salt
organ: a part of the body that does a certain job

Pop It in a Jar

Next, the embalmers made a cut on the left side of the stomach. Through the cut, they removed all the body's organs except the heart. They left the heart because they thought the heart—not the brain—did all the thinking and feeling.

The embalmers then washed the lungs, liver, stomach, and intestines. They put these organs into four canopic jars. The jars were filled with natron. The natron would absorb the water from the organs.

The jars were placed in the tomb, with all the treasures. Carter found such jars in the canopic shrine in Tut's tomb.

intestine: a long tube connected to the stomach that digests food
canopic jar: a large jar that holds the preserved organs of the dead person
absorb: to suck up; take in

Forty Days to Dry

The embalmers stuffed the body with natron. Next, they piled on still more natron until the body was completely covered. Then, they left it to dry for 40 days.

After 40 days, the embalmers emptied the body. They washed it again with water from the Nile. After that, they rubbed the body with scented oils.

A jar for perfumes found in the tomb of King Tut

scented: pleasant smelling

24

Lots of Bandages!

Next the embalmers wrapped the body. They wrapped cloth bandages around the head first. Then they wrapped each finger, toe, arm, and leg.

At this point, they put amulets and jewelry on the body. For a pharaoh like Tut, these amulets and jewels were costly.

The embalmers wrapped a shroud around everything. Then they poured thick, sticky resin over the wrapped mummy. This stopped the body from rotting.

Next, they added more bandages, another shroud, and more resin. There could be as many as seven layers. It took up to 13 days to finish the wrapping. Finally, the embalmers covered the head with a mask. They then put the mummy into a coffin.

---

bandage: a strip of cloth used to cover a piece of the body
amulet: a charm or a piece of jewelry, often with a magic spell or symbol on it, worn to protect the wearer from evil
shroud: a piece of cloth used to wrap a dead body
resin: sap from pine trees

Planning Ahead

Most pharaohs began to plan for their deaths as soon as they became king. A large tomb cannot be built in 70 days. Tombs probably took 40 or more years to build.

Researchers believe that King Tut died unexpectedly. One reason they believe this is that he was not in a pharaoh's tomb. His tomb may have been built for Ay.

A large tomb like the pyramid in the background took many years to build.

researcher: a person who looks for and studies information
unexpectedly: by surprise

Skilled Workers

The pharaohs used Egypt's most skilled workmen to build their tombs. Most of these craftsmen lived in little villages close to where they worked.

Howard Carter found the entrance to King Tut's tomb buried underneath the remains of one of these villages. Diggers thought there would be no more to find under the ancient village ruins. That's why the tomb stayed hidden for so long.

Robbers often raided these ancient tombs. That's why we don't know what other pharaohs had in theirs. This made the discovery of King Tut's tomb so important.

What did the ancient Egyptians expect to find after death? The answer might surprise you.

CHAPTER 4

Life after Death

The ancient Egyptians believed in a life after death. They did rituals to prepare the dead for a new life. What kind of afterlife do you think they believed in?

This painting shows a dead person standing before Osiris.

Judge of the Underworld

Osiris was of one of the most important gods in ancient Egypt. A story told how he came to be king of the underworld.

In the story, Osiris ruled Egypt. He was married to Isis. They had a son named Horus.

Osiris also had a brother named Seth. Seth wanted to rule Egypt. So he tricked Osiris. He had him get into a chest. Seth locked the chest. Then he and his men threw it into the Nile River.

Isis traveled far looking for the chest. Finally, she found it. But before she could bury Osiris, Seth stole the body. He cut it into 14 pieces and hid them all over Egypt. Isis found all the pieces except one.

After 80 years of fighting, Horus defeated Seth and became the new king of the living. Seth became ruler of the deserts. And Osiris became king of the underworld.

---

ritual: a set of actions that is always done in the same way
underworld: the place where the spirits of dead people go

Journey to Judgment

The Egyptians believed that a dead person's soul made a journey to a new life. This happened as soon as the body was buried. But before burial, the dead person's mouth had to be opened. This allowed the dead person to speak at a trial before Osiris.

The dead person's soul followed the sun god through the underworld at night. On the way, it had to get past evil gods, a giant snake, and other horrible monsters.

Embalmers sometimes put a special scroll in the mummy's shroud. This scroll, called *The Book of the Dead,* gave spells and passwords. The soul needed these to enter the Hall of Double Justice.

In the Hall of Double Justice, the soul faced Osiris and 42 other judges. Each of them judged one sin. The soul had to name each judge. It also had to state that it was not guilty of each of these sins.

---

soul: the spiritual part of a person
password: a secret word needed to enter a place

Another Test

If the soul passed this test, it went on to the "Weighing of the Soul." The soul's heart was put on one side of a scale. The feather of truth was put on the other side. The heart and the feather had to balance exactly.

Little Helpers

If the soul passed both these tests, Osiris welcomed it into the Field of Reeds. Here, Osiris gave land to the dead person's soul. It could live there forever. The soul could also return to Earth. There it could enjoy the food offerings left at its tomb.

Once in the Field of Reeds, the soul farmed the land. But there was a way to avoid this work. Most tombs contained ushabti (oo-SHAB-tee) figures. Egyptians believed these little statues did the work for the dead person. King Tut had more than 400 ushabti—365 workers plus 48 overseers.

An ushabti figure from the tomb of King Tut

Reading the Pictures

How did Carter and his team figure out the writing found in the tomb? The ancient Egyptians wrote with hieroglyphs (HIRE-oh-gliffs). In 1799, French archeologists found a very important clue to understanding these hieroglyphs. They discovered the Rosetta Stone.

The Rosetta Stone showed a single message written in two kinds of hieroglyphs and Greek. One archeologist knew the easier hieroglyphs and Greek. So he could then figure out the more difficult hieroglyphs.

hieroglyph: a character used in a system of writing made up of pictures and symbols

Egyptian hieroglyphs

Egyptian demotic, a simpler kind of hieroglyphs

Greek writing

This photo of the Rosetta Stone shows the message carved in three different kinds of writing.

CHAPTER 5

The Curse of the Mummy

"Death shall come on swift wings to him that touches the tomb of Pharaoh." Newspapers claimed this curse was carved on the wall of King Tut's tomb. All who bothered his rest were doomed—or were they?

A mummy found in Egypt

A Real Threat

Tomb robbers were real, however. Robbers twice raided King Tut's tomb after he was buried. The robbers stole jewelry, linens, and make-up. Most of the Tut jewelry we see today came from the mummy itself. The rest was stolen.

Some of the burial workers might have been the robbers. If they were caught, they probably suffered a nasty fate. The ancient Egyptians punished tomb robbers harshly.

Tomb robbers kept stealing anyway. Every other tomb in the Valleys of the Kings and Queens is empty. What happened to all the items stolen from these tombs? Most have never been found. But some of these treasures you can see in American and European museums.

---

fate: what will happen to you
harshly: cruelly

Horror from the Grave

Mummies were popular in horror movies long before Carter found King Tut's tomb. The mummy is one of the three most popular movie monsters. The others are Dracula and Frankenstein. *The Mummy of the King of Ramesses* was the first mummy film, shown in 1910. Since then, filmmakers have made more than 50 mummy movies.

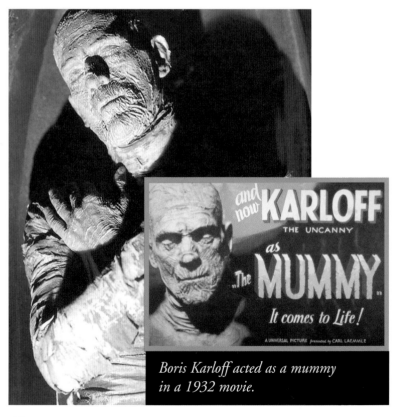

Boris Karloff acted as a mummy in a 1932 movie.

The idea for some of the mummy movies came from a popular story, *Jewel of Seven Stars*. Bram Stoker, author of *Dracula*, wrote this story. It was published in 1903.

In the story, an archeologist gives his daughter an ancient ring. She is then taken over by the spirit of its first owner, an evil Egyptian princess.

Mummies Keep Coming Back

We seem to love the idea of a dead body that comes back to life. The moldy, trailing bandages and the smell of decay only add to the shiver power.

In a way, mummies really don't ever die. Through books, movies, and museums, mummies return—again and again and again!

decay: something rotting
shiver: cold or fearful

Egypt Time Line

B.C.

3100–2686 Early Dynastic Period

2686–2181 The Old Kingdom

2589 Khufu (Cheops) becomes pharaoh and builds the Great Pyramid as his tomb

2181–2040 First Intermediate Period

2040–1650 The Middle Kingdom

1650–1570 Second Intermediate Period

1550–1069 The New Kingdom

1352 Akh-en-Aten becomes pharaoh

1346 Akh-en-Aten moves his capital to Amarna

1336 Akh-en-aten dies; shortly afterward, Tut-ankh-Amun is made pharaoh

1327 Tut-ankh-Amun dies; Ay becomes pharaoh

1323 Ay dies; Hor-em-heb becomes pharaoh

1295 Hor-em-heb dies; end of the 18th Dynasty

1279 Ramesses II becomes pharaoh

1069–747 Third Intermediate Period

747–332 Late Period

332 Alexander the Great conquers Egypt

332–30 Ptolemaic Dynasty

30 Emperor Augustus adds Egypt to the Roman Empire

A.D.

1798 Napoleon Bonaparte and the French army invade Egypt

1799 Rosetta Stone discovered

1822 Jean-François Champollion deciphers the first hieroglyphs

1891 Howard Carter arrives in Egypt for the first time

1907 Lord Carnarvon hires Carter to run his digs

1917 Carter starts digging in the Valley of the Kings

1922 Tomb of Tut-ankh-Amun discovered

The throne of King Tut

Glossary

absorb: to suck up; take in

amulet: a charm or a piece of jewelry, often with a magic spell or symbol on it, worn to protect the wearer from evil

archeology: the study of the past by looking at old buildings and other objects

bandage: a strip of cloth used to cover a piece of the body

burial: the placing of a dead body in its final resting place

burial chamber: a room for a dead body and its coffin

canopic jar: a large jar that holds the preserved organs of the dead person

criminal: a person who breaks the laws of the country

damp: wet or moist

decay: something rotting

dynasty: a series of rulers who belong to the same family

embalmer: in ancient Egypt, a person who makes a mummy

empire: a country ruled by an emperor

exhibition: a public display of works of art or historical objects

fate: what will happen to you

harshly: cruelly

hieroglyph: a character used in a system of writing made up of pictures and symbols

howl: to cry out in pain

intestine: a long tube connected to the stomach that digests food

jackal: a wild animal related to the dog

legend: a story passed down from generation to generation

looted: when valued objects have been stolen from their owners

natron: a natural salt

organ: a part of the body that does a certain job

password: a secret word needed to enter a place

pharaoh: a king of ancient Egypt

researcher: a person who looks for and studies information

resin: sap from pine trees

ritual: a set of actions that is always done in the same way

rubble: a mixture of earth and stones

scented: pleasant smelling

scribe: an educated man who could read and write

shiver: cold or fearful

shrine: any site or structure used in worship or devotion

shroud: a piece of cloth used to wrap a dead body

soul: the spiritual part of a person

tomb: a grave, room, or building for holding a dead body

underworld: the place where the spirits of dead people go

unexpectedly: by surprise

widow: a woman whose husband has died

Bibliography

Berger, Melvin and Gilda Berger. *Mummies of the Pharaohs: Exploring the Valley of the Kings.* Washington, D.C.: National Geographic Society, 2001.

Caselli, Giovanni. *In Search of Tutankhamun: The discovery of a king's tomb.* New York: Peter Bedrick Books, 1999.

Harris, Geraldine. *Ancient Egypt.* Cultural Atlas for Young People. New York: Facts on File, 1990.

Hart, George. *Ancient Egypt.* Eyewitness Books. New York: DK Publishing, 2000.

MacDonald, Fiona. *Ancient Egyptians.* Insights. New York: Barrons Educational Series, Inc., 1993.

Murdoch, David. *Tutankhamun: The Life and Death of a Pharaoh.* DK Discoveries. New York: DK Publishing, 1998.

Reeves, Nicholas. *Into the Mummy's Tomb: The Real-life Discovery of Tutankhamun's Treasures.* A Time Quest Book. New York: Scholastic Inc., 1993.

Useful Addresses

Detroit Institute of Arts
5200 Woodward Avenue
Detroit, MI 48202

Metropolitan Museum of Art
1000 Fifth Avenue
New York, NY 10028–0198

**Phoebe Apperson Hearst Museum
of Anthropology**
University of California
103 Kroeber Hall,
Berkeley, CA 94720–3712

Internet Sites

FactHound offers a safe, fun way to find
Internet sites related to this book. All of the
sites on FactHound have been
researched by our staff.

Here's how:

Visit *www.facthound.com*

FactHound will fetch the best sites for you!

Index